TRANSPORT

· BY DESIGN ·

IAN GRAHAM

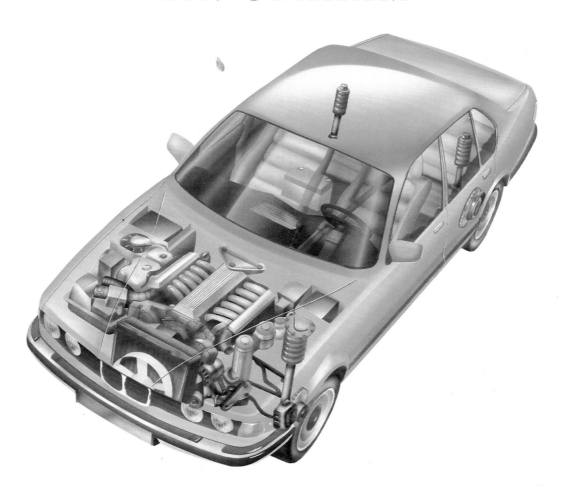

SIMON & SCHUSTER
YOUNG BOOKS

First published in 1994 by
Simon & Schuster Young Books

© 1994 Simon & Schuster Young Books
Campus 400
Maylands Avenue
Hemel Hempstead
Hertfordshire
HP2 7EZ

Managing Editor: Thomas Keegan
Editor: Nicola Barber
Design: David West Children's
Book Design
Illustrators: David Burroughs, Ron Hayward
Associates, David Russell, Simon Tegg,
Ian Thompson.

ISBN 07500 1523 3

A CIP catalogue record for this book is
available from the British Library

Typeset by Goodfellow and Egan Ltd

Printed and bound in Hong Kong

CONTENTS

Cars

People dreamed of building self-propelled vehicles, or automobiles, for centuries, but it was the development of steam engines during the 19th century that led to the first successful cars. These early cars were slow, noisy and smelly. Then, in the 1860s, the discovery of underground oilfields gave engineers a new fuel—petrol. Using petrol, engineers could design more powerful and reliable engines. In 1885, Karl Benz built the first car with a petrol engine.

Cugnot's steamer

The first automobile was a tractor built in 1769 in France by Nicolas-Joseph Cugnot. It was a big, heavy three-wheeled vehicle powered by a steam engine. It could manage a top speed of 3.6km/h for about 20 minutes.

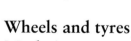

Cugnot's steamer

Wheels and tyres

Modern tyres are made from layers of tough fabric, called plies, encased in rubber. There are two types of tyre. A cross-ply tyre (*right*) is made from plies of fabric with their cords running in different directions. The cords of a radial tyre (*far right*) all run from side-to-side. On top of these cords there are 'breaker belts' running around the tyre for added strength. Most cars have radial tyres.

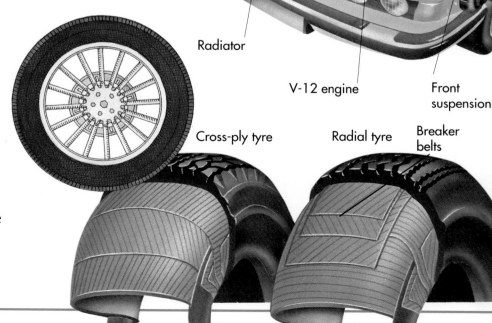

Computer

Radiator

V-12 engine

Front suspension

Cross-ply tyre

Radial tyre

Breaker belts

The gearbox

A car's engine is linked to its road-wheels through a gearbox. The job of the gearbox is to 'gear down' the high speed of the engine to the lower speed needed for the road-wheels. By moving the gear lever, a driver can make a car accelerate smoothly from a walking pace to its top speed.

Gear lever

Gear wheels

Gearbox

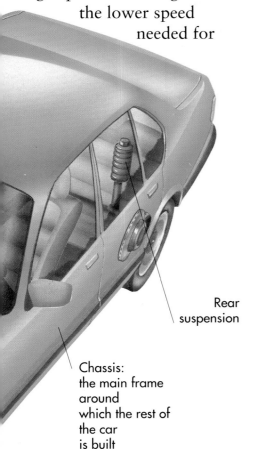

Rear suspension

Chassis:
the main frame around
which the rest of the car
is built

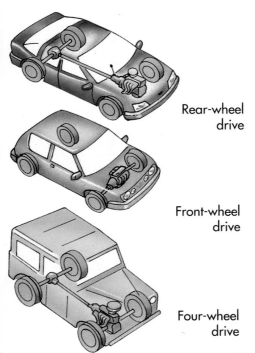

Rear-wheel drive

Front-wheel drive

Four-wheel drive

The modern car

A modern car is more sleek and curved than the earliest cars. The shape of a modern car allows it to cut through the air easily so that fuel is not wasted overcoming air-resistance. Modern engines are heavier and more powerful too. This means that the main frame of the car, its chassis, has to be stronger. Water, cooled by air blowing around a radiator at the front of the car, is constantly pumped around the engine to keep it cool. A springy suspension system makes the ride more comfortable.

Drive combinations

The engines of older cars normally drive the rear wheels, a layout called rear-wheel drive. Most modern cars have front-wheel drive, with the engine driving the two front wheels. Vehicles designed for rough ground have four-wheel drive. With four driven wheels, the vehicle has a better chance of gripping loose surfaces.

Electric cars

One disadvantage of cars fuelled by petrol or diesel oil is that their engines pump out poisonous gases into the atmosphere. Another disadvantage is that reserves of oil will not last forever, and no more oil is being made. Oil is a 'fossil fuel', made many millions of years ago during prehistoric times. One answer is to make cars that do not burn fossil fuels. Electric cars use electricity from batteries to power electric motors that drive the wheels. They are quiet and cause no pollution.

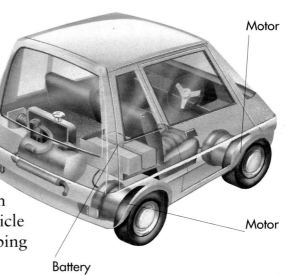

Motor

Motor

Battery

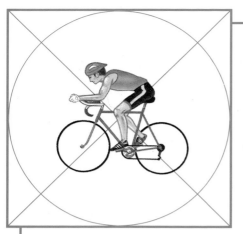

TWO-WHEELED TRANSPORT

Bicycles were developed from two-wheeled machines called hobbyhorses which appeared in the early 19th century. A hobbyhorse was made from a wooden beam that linked two wheels. The rider sat astride the beam and 'walked' the machine along. By the end of the century, the hobbyhorse had been transformed into the bicycle by the addition of pedals, a chain-driven rear wheel, steering and brakes.

Kirkpatrick Macmillan's bicycle

Derailleur gears

The derailleur gear system for bicycles was invented in 1911. When the rider pulls a lever, a selector mechanism pushes the chain sideways so that it slips off one gear-wheel and on to another of a different size.

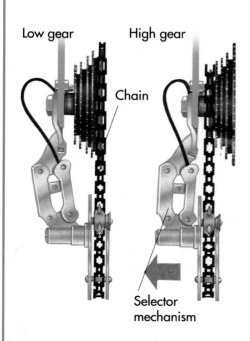

Low gear   High gear

Chain

Selector mechanism

Early bikes

In 1839 a Scottish blacksmith, Kirkpatrick Macmillan, added foot-cranks (like pedals) to a hobbyhorse machine to drive its rear wheels. In 1861, Pierre Michaux added pedals to the front wheel of a hobbyhorse. The first bicycle to have all the features of a modern bike—pedals driving the rear wheel through a chain, wheels the same size and a diamond-shaped frame—was the Rover Safety bike of 1885.

Lotus Superbike

The ultimate bike

At the 1992 Olympic Games, the British cyclist Chris Boardman won a gold medal for the 4000-metre pursuit race. He was riding a revolutionary new bicycle called the Lotus Superbike.

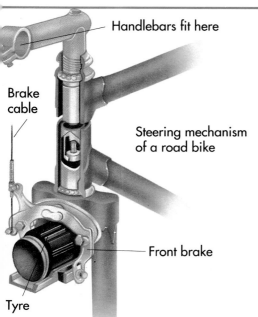

Handlebars fit here

Brake cable

Steering mechanism of a road bike

Front brake

Tyre

The first motorbikes

Steam-powered motorcycles were built as early as the 1860s, but they were not successful. The forerunner of the modern motorcycle was a petrol-engined machine built by Gottlieb Daimler and Wilhelm Maybach in Germany in 1885 (*right*).

Trail bike

Road bike

Moped

Different bikes

There are different types of motorcycles, each designed for different conditions. Road bikes are built to be safe for general use on the roads. Trail bikes are strengthened to ride on rough ground. The tyres on trail bikes have a coarse tread to grip muddy surfaces. Mopeds are motorized bicycles suitable for short trips in towns.

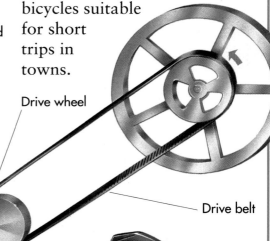

Drive wheel

Drive belt

The mountain bike

Mountain bikes are built more sturdily than other bikes so that they can withstand the extra stresses, strains and vibrations of being ridden on mountain tracks and rough ground. The first mountain bikes were built in the early 1970s by cyclists in California, USA. These cyclists strengthened their own bikes so that they could be ridden on nearby mountain slopes. Mountain bikes proved to be so popular that bicycle manufacturers started to make them.

Belt drive

The power of a motorcycle's engine has to be transferred to its rear wheel. The first bikes used a belt, but it tended to slip. Chains replaced belts, but today toothed rubber belts are often used.

Today's bike

A modern racing bike (*right*) is streamlined to minimize air-resistance. Its tyres are broad and made from soft rubber to grip the track. The fastest racing bike can reach speeds of more than 200 km/h.

TRUCKS AND BUSES

There has always been a need to transport raw materials and goods from the people who make them to the people who want them. For public transport there is a need for vehicles that can carry people. Until the 1920s, buses were made by building a bus body on to a truck chassis. The first purpose-built buses were made in the United States. They had a lower chassis than a truck to make it easier for people to get in and out.

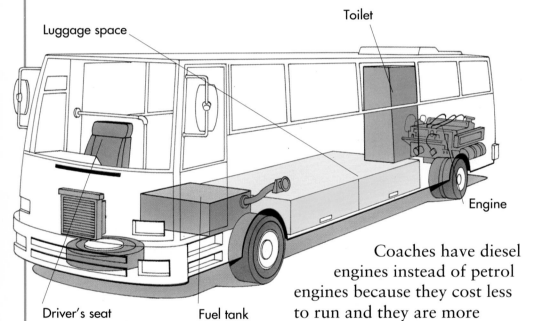

Luggage space

Toilet

Engine

Driver's seat

Fuel tank

Coaches have diesel engines instead of petrol engines because they cost less to run and they are more reliable.

The modern coach
The modern coach is a spacious vehicle with comfortable seats and large windows. An air-conditioning system keeps the passengers cool in hot weather and warm when it is cold outside. There is a compartment under the floor for storing luggage. A powerful diesel engine is tucked away at the back.

Trams and trolleys
Trams are buses that run on rails in the road. Trolley buses did not run on rails, so they could be steered to either side of the overhead wires that supplied their motors with electricity.

Road buses
The manufacturers of early motor buses experimented with different layouts. One layout looked rather like a train, with a truck that carried luggage pulling a passenger trailer (*left*).

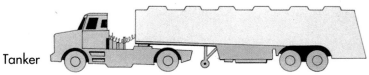

Tanker

Articulated and rigid

Small trucks have a rigid chassis linking the driver's cab to the rest of the truck. Longer trucks bend in the middle to allow them to get round corners more easily. These are called articulated trucks. Animals such as lobsters are articulated too.

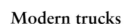
Articulated

Rigid

Lobster

Modern trucks

Today, trucks are more streamlined than they used to be. They are designed like this so that they cut through the air more easily. Some trucks have an angled panel above the cab to deflect air smoothly over the trailer.

Power-assisted steering

To help the driver, modern trucks are usually equipped with power-assisted steering. When the driver turns the steering wheel, a pump forces oil down a pipe. The oil pushes a piston down a cylinder. The piston is fixed to the wheels, so when it moves, the wheels turn.

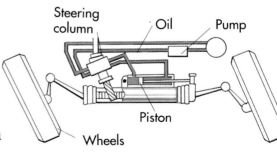
Steering column
Oil
Pump
Piston
Wheels

Different types

Trucks are shaped for the jobs they do. Tankers tow a container for carrying liquids. Vans have a covered goods compartment. Car transporters have two decks. Dump trucks tip up to let a loose load slide out through a swing-door at the back.

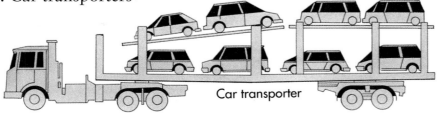
Van
Car transporter

Dump truck

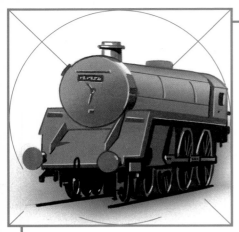

TRAINS

The invention of the train made it possible to carry hundreds of passengers over long distances in a single vehicle. But the idea of transporting loads in vehicles on rails is not a new one. In 1550, horse-drawn wagons running on rails were used for mining at Leberthal in Alsace, France. Mines in Britain also used rail wagons from the early 1600s. Rails were used because it was easier to haul a heavy load on smooth rails than over rough ground. The first railway engines were powered by steam. Today, they have been replaced almost everywhere by electric and diesel engines.

The *Rocket*

The *Mallard*
On July 3rd 1938 a streamlined locomotive called *Mallard* set a world record speed for steam engines of 201.16km/h. The *Mallard* weighed 244 tonnes and was pulling seven coaches. The record still stand unbeaten today.

The *Rocket*
In 1829, a competition was held to find the most reliable railway locomotive. It was won by the *Rocket*, a locomotive built by George Stephenson and his son Robert. The *Rocket* could manage a top speed of 56km/h.

Mallard

Diesel hydraulic

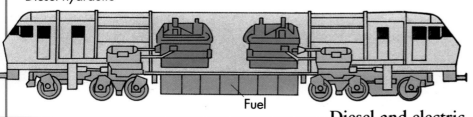

Fuel

Diesel and electric
Electric trains use overhead power cables or electrified track. In diesel-electric trains, a diesel engine powers a generator which produces electricity to drive the wheels. Diesel-hydraulic locomotives use a diesel engine to power a hydraulic pump. The pump forces oil through a turbine, making it spin. The turbine is connected to the wheels which also turn.

Electric Transformers

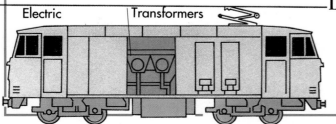

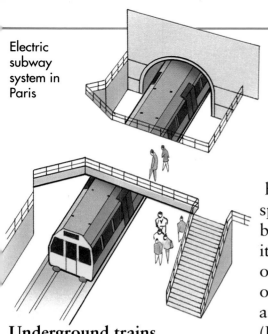

Electric subway system in Paris

Underground trains
Travelling across a busy city can be difficult and time-consuming because of traffic jams. One answer is to build a railway system underground. The trains travel on rails through underground tunnels. Cities with underground railway systems include New York, London, Paris and Moscow. The system in London is the largest in the world. If all of its routes were laid end-to-end, they would be 409km long.

Cable

The TGV
Passengers in France regularly travel on the world's fastest train, the Train à Grande Vitesse or TGV, meaning 'high-speed train'. In test runs, the TGV has reached record-breaking speeds of more than 500km/h, but with passengers on board it travels at an average speed of 220km/h. Like the world's other high-speed trains, such as the Japanese Shinkansen (Bullet) train, the TGV is an electric train.

It collects electricity from wires hung above the track by means of a pantograph. This is a frame that is pushed up from the train's roof until it touches the overhead wires.

Pantograph

TGV

Funicular railways
Funicular railways are built up steep hillsides, especially at seaside resorts. Two cars are linked by cable. When the cable is wound by a motor, the top car descends and the lower car is pulled up.

Maglev
The trains of the future will fly just above the track at up to 500km/h, supported by magnetic fields. To propel the train forwards, magnets in the track ahead of the train attract it and those behind repel it.

Guideway magnets

Boats

Ten thousand years ago, people made boats from materials that floated naturally. They tied tree trunks together to make rafts; or hollowed out trunks to form dugout canoes. In places where there were few trees, they collected tall grassy reeds from the water's edge and tied them into bundles to make reed boats. Where there were neither trees nor reeds, boats were made by stretching animal skins over frames. These early boats were propelled by oars or by poles pushed into the river bed. Boats such as these are still used in many parts of the world.

Early rowing boats
Early warships were powered by banks of rowers. This allowed the warships to go in any direction at any time.

Sometimes sails were used as well, when the wind was blowing in the right direction.

Water-boatman

Coracles
The coracle is an ancient boat from Ireland and Wales. It was made by stretching an animal skin over a light frame. The frame was built out of strips of wood tied together with grass. The coracle was steered and propelled by one oar, moved in a side-to-side, stirring action.

Paddle blade

Shaft

The native American canoe

Many native Americans made canoes by covering a wooden frame with animal skins or waterproof tree bark. They propelled their canoes by kneeling inside and pulling against the water with broad paddles. The size of a dugout canoe was limited by the size of available tree trunks, but a frame canoe could be almost any size.

Native American canoe

Effort

Load

Fulcrum

How a lever works

The modern rowing boat

The modern rowing boat is powered by oars called sculls. A scull is a lever. Most levers have a fulcrum in the middle and the effort and load at opposite ends. The oar is different. When the rower pulls at one end of the oar, the broad blade catches in the water. The blade becomes a pivot, and a force is applied to the boat, propelling it backwards. The water-boatman moves around in a similar way.

Venetian gondola

Gondolas and punts

Gondolas are the traditional boats of Venice. Punts are propelled by a pole pushed into the river bed.

Seat

Scull

Punt

Modern canoes

Most modern canoes are made from polyethylene (a plastic) in one of two ways. A blob of molten plastic is blown up like a balloon inside a mould. Alternatively, plastic granules are melted inside a mould. Paddles have fibreglass or carbon fibre blades at the ends of aluminium or carbon fibre shafts.

Blade

Bow

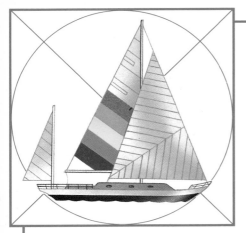

SAILING SHIPS

The first sailing boats date back to about 3000BC. These boats had square sails which meant they could move only in the same direction as the wind. In about AD100, Arab sailors found that by setting a triangular 'lateen' sail at an angle to the wind they could sail in almost any direction. The golden age of sail was the 19th century, when large, fast 'clippers' travelled the trade routes of the world.

Lateen sail

The lateen sail
Arab sailors developed the lateen sail because, in the intense heat of the region, rowers soon became exhausted. The lateen sail allowed boats to keep going under wind power, even if the wind was blowing in the wrong direction.

Different hulls
The outrigger canoe was developed thousands of years ago in the South Pacific. An outrigger is a piece of wood running parallel to the hull of a canoe, attached by two or more booms. The outrigger helps to make the canoe more stable. The twin-hulled catamaran and three-hulled trimaran come from the South Pacific too. In the 15th century, boats were first fitted with centre-boards to stop them sliding sideways. In 1840, the centre-board became part of the keel of large yachts, forming a fin keel.

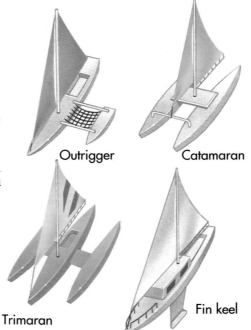

Outrigger

Catamaran

Trimaran

Fin keel

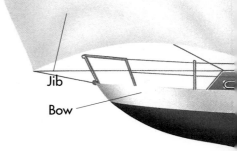

Jib

Bow

The modern sailing yacht
Most yachts have at least two sails, one (a jib) ahead of the mast and another (the mainsail) behind it. A small mizzen sail is sometimes hung from a short mast behind the main mast. When the yacht is sailing in the same direction as the wind, an enormous sail

How sails work

When the wind blows against a sail it fills the sail with air. The air that is pushed out around the front of the sail has to travel further and faster than air flowing across the back. Fast-moving air has a lower pressure than slow-moving air so there is low pressure in front of the sail, and high pressure behind it. The result is that the sail is sucked forwards. The Portuguese man-of-war jellyfish is blown along by a sail too.

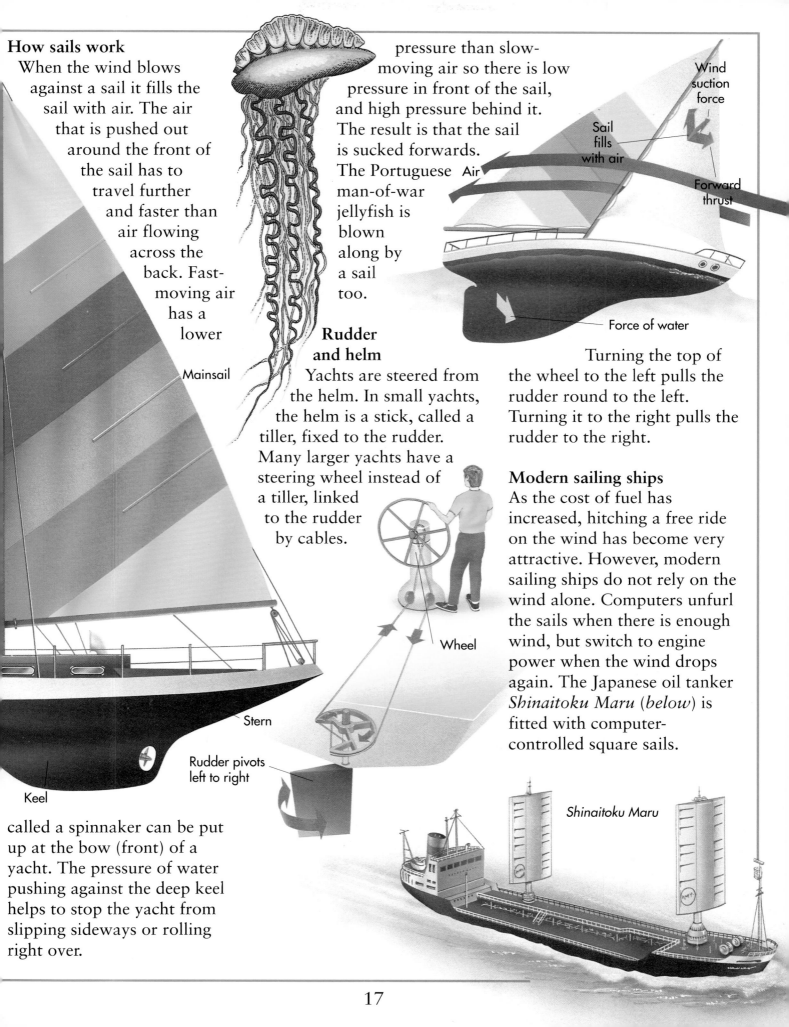

Mainsail

Wind suction force

Sail fills with air

Air

Forward thrust

Force of water

Keel

Stern

Rudder pivots left to right

Wheel

Shinaitoku Maru

Rudder and helm

Yachts are steered from the helm. In small yachts, the helm is a stick, called a tiller, fixed to the rudder. Many larger yachts have a steering wheel instead of a tiller, linked to the rudder by cables. Turning the top of the wheel to the left pulls the rudder round to the left. Turning it to the right pulls the rudder to the right.

Modern sailing ships

As the cost of fuel has increased, hitching a free ride on the wind has become very attractive. However, modern sailing ships do not rely on the wind alone. Computers unfurl the sails when there is enough wind, but switch to engine power when the wind drops again. The Japanese oil tanker *Shinaitoku Maru* (*below*) is fitted with computer-controlled square sails.

called a spinnaker can be put up at the bow (front) of a yacht. The pressure of water pushing against the deep keel helps to stop the yacht from slipping sideways or rolling right over.

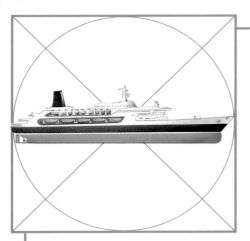

SHIPS

Ships are large, sea-going vessels that carry passengers or cargo. All ships were propelled by the wind until the middle of the 19th century. By then, steam engines were being installed in ships. The first steamships were propelled by paddle wheels, but they were soon replaced by the screw propeller. At the same time, iron began to be used instead of wood as a ship-building material. Its greater strength made it possible to build much bigger ships. By the 1880s, steel was replacing iron because it was stronger and more easily shaped.

Paddle wheel

Paddle wheel

Paddle wheels and propellers
The argument about which was more powerful—the screw propeller or the paddle wheel—was finally settled in 1845 with a tug of war between HMS *Rattler* and HMS *Alecto*. The propeller-driven *Rattler* won easily.

The screw propeller
The job of the propeller is to transmit the power of a ship's engine to the water. When the propeller moves, its angled blades spin through the water like a screw screwing into wood. This screw action draws water from ahead of the propeller and pushes it backwards. The water pushes against the blades and this force propels the ship forwards.

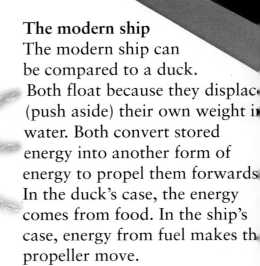

Tanker

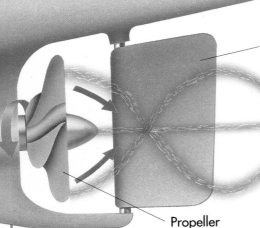

Rudder

Propeller

Ship forced through water

The modern ship
The modern ship can be compared to a duck. Both float because they displace (push aside) their own weight in water. Both convert stored energy into another form of energy to propel them forwards. In the duck's case, the energy comes from food. In the ship's case, energy from fuel makes the propeller move.

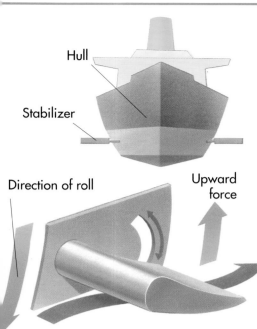

Hull

Stabilizer

Direction of roll

Upward force

Stabilizers

The rolling action of a ship in rough seas can make passengers seasick or, at worst,

Duck

overturn the ship. In the 1930s, devices called stabilizers were developed to reduce the rolling motion of a ship in a storm. They consisted of fins either side of the hull which were linked to gyroscopes. The gyroscope is a spinning wheel that tries to stay in the same position even when the ship moves around it. When the ship begins to roll, the gyroscope detects this movement and automatically adjusts the angle of the fin to try to stop the roll.

Different ships

Specialized ships have been developed to carry different cargoes. Ro-ros have bow and stern ramps so that passengers can drive straight on to the ship. Barges are narrow, flat-bottomed ships for carrying loads in rivers and canals. Gas containers carry gas in pressurized tanks. Bulk carriers transport large amounts of cargo in huge holds. Oil tankers carry crude oil around the world.

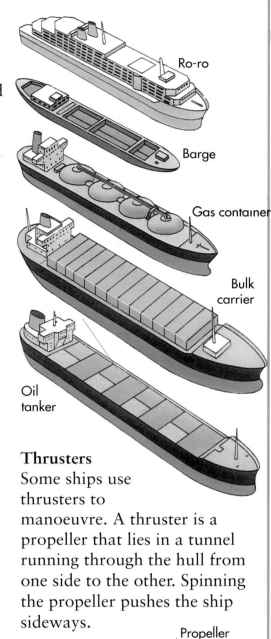

Ro-ro

Barge

Gas container

Bulk carrier

Oil tanker

Thrusters

Some ships use thrusters to manoeuvre. A thruster is a propeller that lies in a tunnel running through the hull from one side to the other. Spinning the propeller pushes the ship sideways.

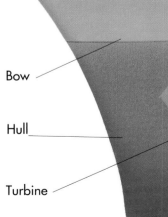

Propeller

Bow

Hull

Turbine

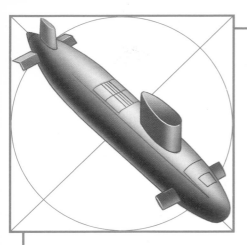

SUBMARINES

People tried to build submarines as long ago as the 17th century. These early submarines didn't work very well because there were no suitable engines to power them. The invention of the internal combustion engine in the 19th century provided a more suitable source of power. Today, the use of nuclear power has made a new breed of submarines possible—big, deep-diving and able to stay under the sea for months at a time.

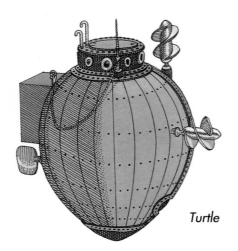

Turtle

Turtle and *Nautilus*

In 1776, an underwater craft called the *Turtle* attacked the English ship *Eagle* outside New York harbour during the American War of Independence. In 1798, another American, Robert Fulton, built the *Nautilus*, the first submarine to have a metal hull.

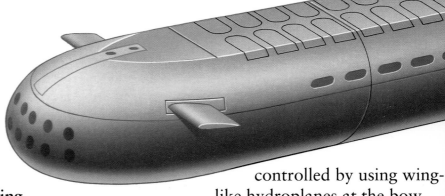

Conning tower

A submarine's conning tower, also called the fin or sail, contains periscopes and masts for sensing and communicating with the outside world. The masts include radio, radar and electronic warfare (EW) aerials.

Wireless mast

EW mast

Attack periscope

Radar mast

Navigation platform

Steering

Submarines are steered to the left and right by a rudder that works in the same way as a ship's rudder. Movement up and down in the water is controlled by using wing-like hydroplanes at the bow and stern. When the hydroplanes are tilted, water pushes against them and tips the submarine nose-up or -down.

Diving

Turning right

Rising

Submarines

A submarine's hull is shaped so that it can slip through the water silently. The streamlined outer hull covers an inner pressure hull designed to withstand the crushing force of water when the submarine dives. Until the 1950s, submarines were long and thin, but they could be difficult to control underwater. The US Navy designed a new hull shaped like a killer whale. It was easier to control underwater at all speeds. Submarines have grown in size since then. The biggest submarine ever built is the Russian *Typhoon* class. These giant vessels are 170 metres long.

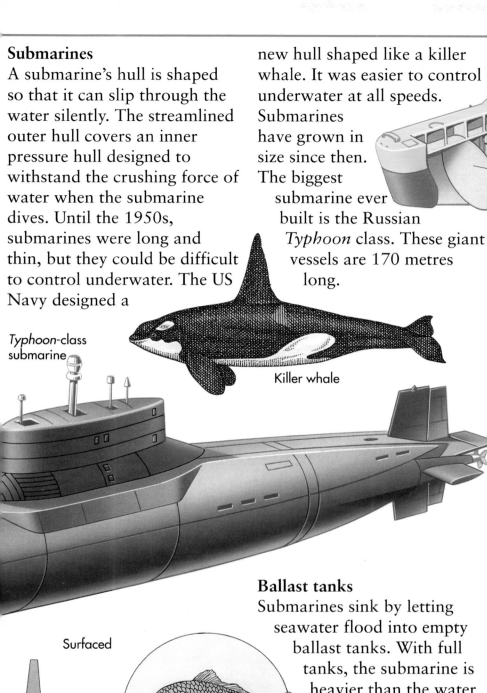

Typhoon-class submarine

Killer whale

Iron ballast

Entrance

Hull filled with petrol

Steel sphere

The *Trieste*

The deepest dive by a manned craft was made by the bathyscaphe *Trieste* on 23 January 1960. It descended 10,916 metres into Challenger Deep in the Marianas Trench in the Pacific Ocean. It then dropped its iron ballast and started back to the surface.

Submersibles

Submarines operate on their own, independent of any surface ship. But there are smaller craft, called submersibles, that are carried out to sea by a ship. One example of a submersible is *Alvin*, the craft that explored the wreck of the *Titanic* on the bottom of the Atlantic Ocean.

Surfaced

Diving

Surfacing again

Ballast tanks

Submarines sink by letting seawater flood into empty ballast tanks. With full tanks, the submarine is heavier than the water around it and it sinks. To come back to the surface, air is forced into the ballast tanks, pushing the water out. The submarine becomes lighter than the water around it and floats up to the surface. Many fish also control their depth by inflating or deflating a balloon-like swim bladder.

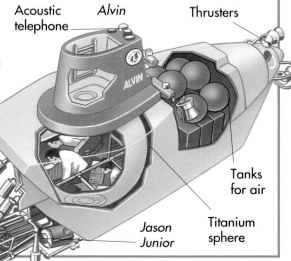

Acoustic telephone

Alvin

Thrusters

ALVIN

Tanks for air

Jason Junior

Titanium sphere

ABOVE THE WAVES

All boats and ships experience a force called drag that tries to slow them down. Drag is caused by the water pulling against the hull. If drag could be reduced, boats and ships would be able to reach much higher speeds because they would not waste wind or fuel power in overcoming drag. Several types of sea-going vessels solve this problem by lifting their hulls out of the water at high speeds. The hovercraft, hydrofoil and airfoil all do this, but in different ways.

SRN1

Early hovercraft
The first hovercraft was a seven-tonne prototype called SRN1 designed by a British engineer, Sir Christopher Cockerell. Its first flight was on May 30th 1959. It reached a speed of 100km/h.

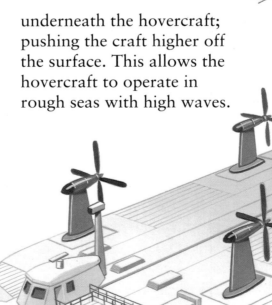

Propeller

Lift fan

Gas turbine engine

Flexible skirt

SRN4

The modern hovercraft
Modern hovercraft are many times bigger than the tiny SRN1. The world's largest hovercraft is the SRN4. The 300-tonne craft is 56 metres long and it can carry 418 passengers and 60 cars. It has four jet engines, each driving a four-bladed propeller, which push the SRN4 along at more than 120km/h. The same engines also drive lift fans hidden inside the hovercraft's body which push the hovercraft up. A flexible skirt holds the air cushion in place underneath the hovercraft; pushing the craft higher off the surface. This allows the hovercraft to operate in rough seas with high waves.

Jet-ski

In the 1960s, Clayton Jacobson designed a new type of vehicle, the jet-ski. The jet-ski combines the thrills and skills of water-skiing and motorcycling. It skims across the water's surface by sucking water in and blowing it out as a jet at the back.

Hydrofoils

At low speeds, a hydrofoil (*below*) looks like any other boat. But when it accelerates the underwater foils work like wings and produce lift. The hydrofoil rises up out of the water. The first designs had ladder foils, then surface piercing foils. In both cases, if the boat sank too low more of the foil was submerged, immediately creating more lift. Depth-effect and submerged foils lie under the water, free from turbulence. This gives a smoother ride.

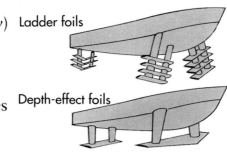

Ladder foils

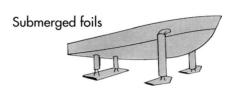

Depth-effect foils

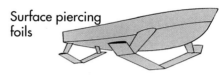

Submerged foils

Surface piercing foils

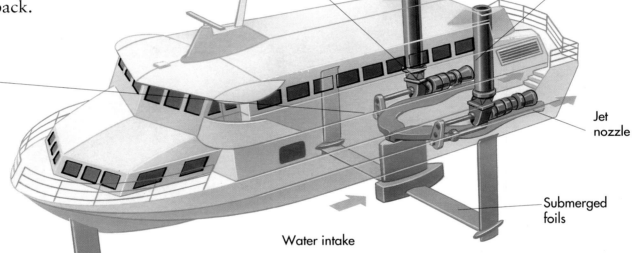

Turbine

Turbine exhaust

Jet water pump

Jet nozzle

Submerged foils

Water intake

Airfoil

The airfoil is an experimental craft being developed in Germany. It rides on an air cushion like a hovercraft, but it uses wings instead of fans to make the cushion. As the airfoil accelerates, its short wings create lift. As the boat rises, air flowing underneath the wings is compressed to form a high-pressure cushion. The vehicle hugs the water's surface. As all the engine power goes into propulsion, airfoils should be capable of higher speeds than hovercraft.

Magnetic boats

Japanese researchers believe that a boat can be propelled by magnets! Powerful magnets inside the hull repel magnetic fields around the boat, driving it forwards.

AEROPLANES

There was little progress in making flying machines until the Englishman Sir George Cayley laid down the mathematical principles of flight in the early 19th century. In 1853, he made a glider big enough to carry his coachman. In Germany in the 1890s, Otto Lilienthal was also making and flying gliders. Meanwhile in the United States, Orville Wright and his brother Wilbur were using kites and gliders to learn how to control an aircraft in flight. They then made their own engine and propellers, and built a powered aeroplane, the *Flyer 1*. It became the first aeroplane to fly, on 17 December 1903.

Early monoplane

Triplane

Monoplane

Development

In the early years of aviation, planes with two or three pairs of wings were more popular than monoplanes. But later monoplane designs produced less air-resistance.

Radar

Flight deck

Nose wheel

First class cabin

Wings

The shape of a plane's wings depends on the speed for which it is designed. The slowest propeller planes (A) have wings that stretch straight out from the plane's fuselage (body). Faster planes like the jumbo jet (B) have slightly swept-back wings. The fastest planes, like the supersonic airliner *Concorde* (C), have wings swept back so much that they form a triangular 'delta' shape. Some military aircraft that have to operate at both low and supersonic speeds have moveable wings (D).

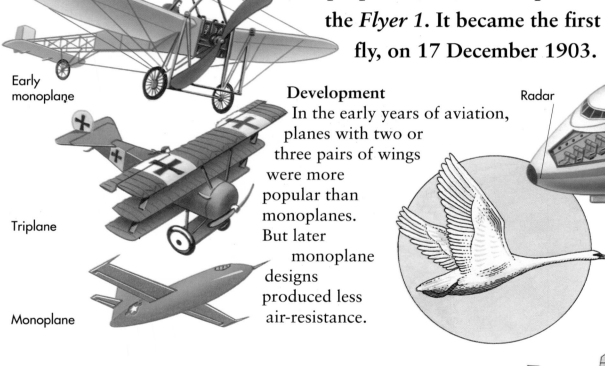

A

B

C

D

The modern airliner

A modern airliner such as the Boeing 747 jumbo jet thunders down the runway in order to pick up enough speed for take-off. A swan also has to run fast across the water to take off. At about 300km/h, the wings of a jumbo jet lift the 350-tonne aircraft into the air. It then accelerates to its cruising speed of 900km/h. Inside the plane, a sealed cabin allows up to 400 passengers to travel half way round the world in comfort. Satellites and radio are used to keep the jumbo jet on course.

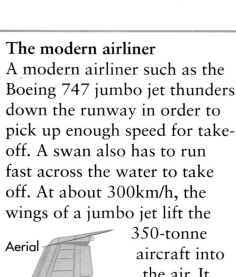

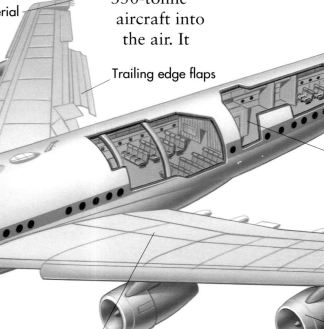

Aerial

Trailing edge flaps

Galley

Outer aileron

Elevator

Yaw

Pitch

Roll

Turbofan

Fuel tanks

Controls

An aeroplane is steered by moving three sets of panels called control surfaces—the rudder in the vertical fin, the elevators in the tailplane and the ailerons in the wings. Turning the rudder steers the plane to the left or right (yaw). Tilting the elevators tips the nose of the plane up or down (pitch). And to make the plane roll, the ailerons are tilted in opposite directions.

Flight deck

The instruments and controls used to fly an airliner are housed on the flight deck in the front of the plane. There are instrument panels in front of the two pilots, on the floor between them and in the ceiling.

Concorde

Concorde's needle-like shape helps it to cut through the air at Mach 2, twice the speed of sound. Its nose is so long that it has to be swivelled down for take-off and landing, so that the pilot can see the runway.

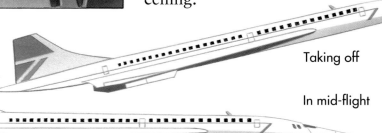

Taking off

In mid-flight

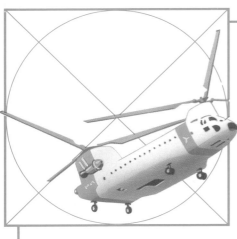

HELICOPTERS

The rotor blades of a helicopter act like wings, creating lift as they cut through the air. A small rotor in the tail stops the helicopter spinning in the opposite direction to its main rotor. Rotor blades produce lift even when the helicopter is standing still. This means that the helicopter can take off vertically and hover. If a helicopter's engines fail, it sinks to the ground like a sycamore seed—nature's own 'helicopter'.

Tailplane

Tail rotor

Early helicopters

The first helicopters were built in the early 1900s, but they could barely lift themselves off the ground. The modern helicopter was developed in the 1930s by Igor Sikorsky. His VS-300, one of the first practical helicopters to fly, had the layout still used by helicopters today—a main overhead rotor and a small tail rotor. Helicopters grew in popularity in the 1950s after a new type of reliable and powerful engine, the turboshaft, was developed.

Sycamore seed

Steering a helicopter

A helicopter is steered by tilting the rotor disc. The pilot pushes a lever to make the swash plate in the rotor head tilt to one side. This changes the angle of the rotor blades as they pass over the swash plate. The extra lift on one side steers the helicopter to the right or left.

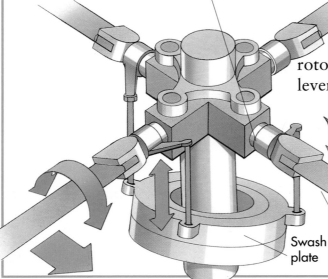

Blade tilts

Blade

Swash plate

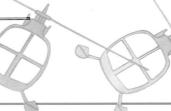

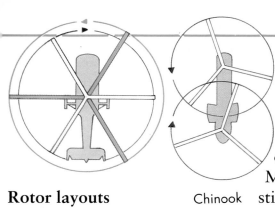

Rotor layouts

Chinook

Most helicopters have one overhead main rotor, but the Chinook transport helicopter has two. The Chinook doesn't need a tail rotor because the overhead rotors cancel out each other's turning forces.

Flight controls

Engine speed is controlled by the throttle control. Height is controlled by raising or lowering the collective pitch lever. Moving the cyclic control stick in any direction makes the helicopter fly in that direction.

Cyclic control stick

Collective pitch lever

Throttle

Directional control pedals

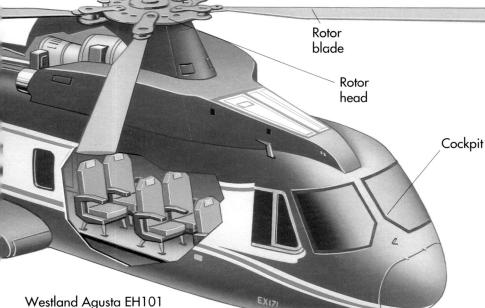

Rotor blade

Rotor head

Cockpit

Westland Agusta EH101

Different jobs

Helicopters perform many different jobs including spraying crops, air-sea rescue, transporting cargoes and passengers, and military work.

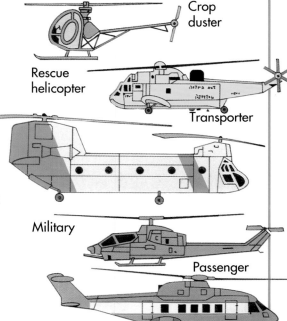

Crop duster

Rescue helicopter

Transporter

Military

Passenger

The helicopter

The Westland Agusta EH101 is a typical example of a modern helicopter. It can cruise at 278km/h and carry 30 passengers a distance of up to 1000km. A computer monitors vibrations in its structure and instantly produces vibrations in the opposite direction. The two sets of vibrations cancel each other out, making the EH101 quieter inside than other helicopters. Its five main rotor blades and tail rotor are powered by three turboshaft engines. If one engine fails, the helicopter can still fly safely using only two engines.

CONTROLLED FALLING

Gliders, hang-gliders and parachutes all provide a way of controlling someone's fall to earth, but they do it in different ways. The parachute works by producing so much drag (air-resistance) that it slows the parachutist's fall to a safe speed. The wings of a glider create lift, slowing its descent. The hang-glider is a combination of both a kite and a glider.

Air escaping

Air fills canopy

Steering lines

Parachuting

Leonardo da Vinci's many plans and sketches for inventions include a pyramid-shaped parachute, but it was probably never constructed. The first recorded parachute jumps were made at the end of the 18th century. The first from an aeroplane was made in 1912. During World War II soldiers were sometimes delivered to battlefields by parachute. In peace time, parachute jumping has become a popular leisure activity. When a parachutist jumps out of a plane, the parachute fills with

Hang-gliders

The hang-glider wing was developed in the 1950s by Professor Francis Rogallo. The hang-glider pilot, suspended underneath the fabric canopy, takes off by running down a hillside. The canopy fills with air,

forming an aerofoil shape and creating lift. The pilot steers by shifting to the side to tilt the wing.

The weight of the parachutist pulls downwards, but it is opposed by the drag of the parachute which acts upwards, slowing the descent.

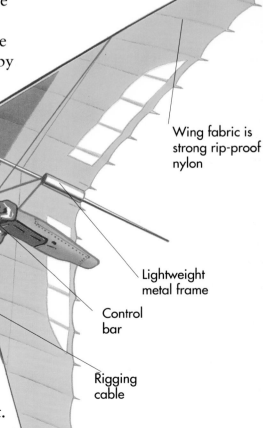

Wing fabric is strong rip-proof nylon

Lightweight metal frame

Control bar

Rigging cable

Thermals

Air that is warmed by the ground produces columns of rising air called thermals. Birds circle inside thermals to soar upwards. Gliders use thermals in the same way.

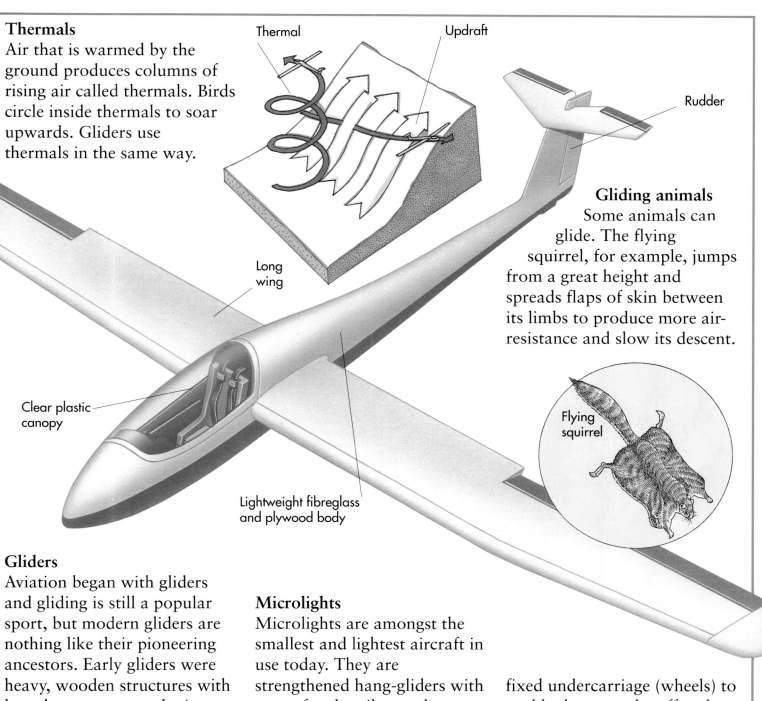

Thermal

Updraft

Rudder

Long wing

Gliding animals
Some animals can glide. The flying squirrel, for example, jumps from a great height and spreads flaps of skin between its limbs to produce more air-resistance and slow its descent.

Flying squirrel

Clear plastic canopy

Lightweight fibreglass and plywood body

Gliders

Aviation began with gliders and gliding is still a popular sport, but modern gliders are nothing like their pioneering ancestors. Early gliders were heavy, wooden structures with broad canvas-covered wings. Modern gliders are slender, streamlined craft made from fibreglass and plastic. Their narrow wings are efficient for gliding. Birds that spend a lot of time gliding, such as the albatross, also have long, thin wings.

Microlights

Microlights are amongst the smallest and lightest aircraft in use today. They are strengthened hang-gliders with a seat for the pilot, and an engine and a propeller suspended underneath. They also have a simple fixed undercarriage (wheels) to enable them to take off and land with the pilot seated. They have fabric-covered wings like a hang-glider, and an open fuselage. The microlight shown here has a small rudder at the end of each wing, elevators at the front for pitch control, and roll spoilers in the wings to make the aircraft roll.

Engine

Frame

AIRSHIPS & BALLOONS

Manned flight began with the balloon. There were two types of early balloon. One type generated lift by heating the air inside the balloon by means of a fire suspended underneath. The other type, the gas balloon, was filled with a gas that was lighter than air—hydrogen. Both types were dangerous. The fire in the hot-air balloon could easily set light to the balloon. The hydrogen used in gas balloons was also highly flammable. Modern airships are now filled with safe helium gas.

The modern airship

Modern airships are filled with helium gas. Helium is heavier than hydrogen, but still lighter than air. Its advantage is that it doesn't burn. New materials and modern engines make the modern airship much safer and more reliable.

Hot air rises

Cold air sinks

Air bags

An airship's height is controlled by bags called 'ballonets'. The airship is filled with helium, so if air is let out of the ballonets the airship becomes lighter than the surrounding air and it rises. If the engines pump air back into the ballonets, the airship becomes heavier again, and it descends.

The first balloons

The first hot-air balloons were made in France in the 1780s by the Montgolfier brothers, Joseph and Jacques. On 15 October 1783, Pilâtre de Rozier and the Marquis d'Arlandes lifted off in a Montgolfier balloon. For the first few flights, the balloon was tied to the ground. But on 21 November 1783, the same passengers made the first free flight. It lasted 25 minutes.

Going up

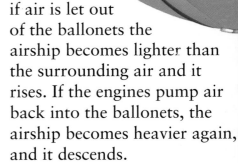

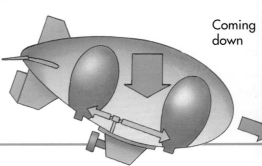

Coming down

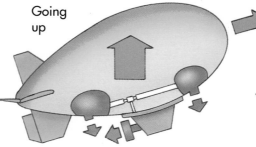

The basket

Balloon baskets are traditionally made from wickerwork (woven twigs). This material is used because it is strong and flexible, bending and moving to absorb the stresses and strains of flight.

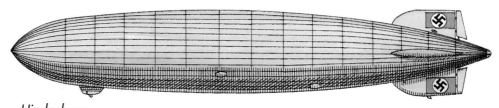

Hindenburg

Early airships

The airship was invented in 1852 when Henri Giffard hung a steam engine under a hydrogen balloon. In the early 1900s, Count Ferdinand von Zeppelin began to build airships. The biggest of these were the *Graf Zeppelin II* and the *Hindenburg*.

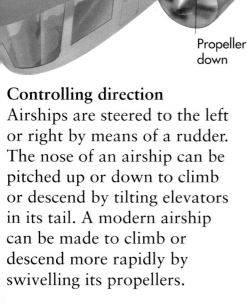

Elevator

Air ballonet

Air ballonet

Propeller down

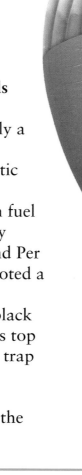

Fly Virgin

Controlling direction

Airships are steered to the left or right by means of a rudder. The nose of an airship can be pitched up or down to climb or descend by tilting elevators in its tail. A modern airship can be made to climb or descend more rapidly by swivelling its propellers.

New materials

In theory, it is impossible to fly a hot-air balloon across the Atlantic Ocean because it cannot carry enough fuel to stay aloft. But in July 1987, Richard Branson and Per Lindstrand successfully piloted a hot-air balloon across the ocean. Its lower half was black to absorb the sun's heat. Its top half was silver-coloured to trap the heat inside. This solar-heating effect reduced the amount of fuel needed for the crossing.

PISTON ENGINES

Engines are the driving force of modern transport. The first engines to be developed were steam engines. Heat produced by burning fuel outside the engine turned water into steam. The expanding steam was then used to push pistons down cylinders. At the end of the 19th century the internal combustion engine was invented. It burns its fuel, petrol, inside the engine.

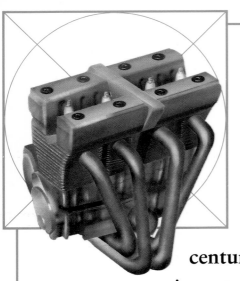

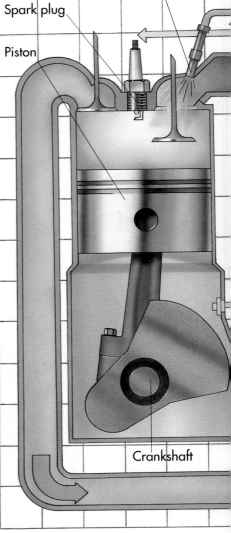

Fuel injector

Spark plug

Piston

Crankshaft

Steam locomotive

In a steam locomotive, coal or wood is burned to heat water in the boiler. The steam from the boiling water is piped into a cylinder to move a piston. The to-and-fro motion of the piston is used to turn the wheels.

Boiler

Steam and smoke

Pistons

Two-stroke

The simplest type of internal combustion engine is called a two-stroke engine. On the upward stroke, fuel and air are sucked into the cylinder. The final part of the upstroke squashes, or compresses the fuel-air mixture. The mixture is ignited, and as it burns it expands and pushes the piston down. The final part of the downstroke pushes waste gases out of the cylinder.

Upstroke
Fuel-air in

Downstroke
Fuel ignites

Upstroke
Piston squashes fuel-air mixture

Downstroke
Gases out

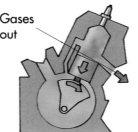

Internal combustion

A car engine is a complicated machine. Valves must open and close at exactly the right moments to let fuel in and waste gases out. Spark plugs

Wankel engine

A car engine works by making pistons move to-and-fro inside cylinders. But the pistons drive wheels that rotate. It would be simpler if the pistons rotated like the wheels. One successful 'rotary engine' has been built. It is the Wankel engine, developed by Felix Wankel between 1938 and 1964. It

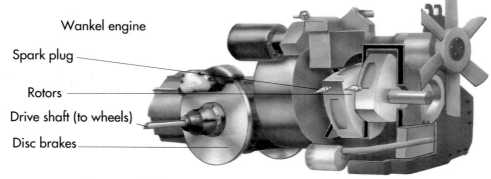

Wankel engine
Spark plug
Rotors
Drive shaft (to wheels)
Disc brakes

uses two three-sided pistons, called rotors. As each rotor spins round inside its housing, the space between it and the housing expands and shrinks, just like the fuel space in the cylinders of a piston engine.

Air in
Computer
Turbine
Air in
Turbocharger
Exhaust gases

must make sparks to ignite the fuel-air mixture. More advanced engines have turbochargers to increase the air pressure in the engine, producing more power.

Four-stroke

The first downstroke of a four-stroke engine sucks fuel and air into the cylinder. The first upstroke compresses the mixture. When the mixture is ignited, it expands and pushes the piston down. Finally, the second upstroke pushes the waste gases out of the cylinder. The four-stroke cycle was invented by Nikolaus Otto in 1876. Karl Benz made the first petrol-fed four-stroke engine in 1885.

Diesel

The diesel engine was invented in 1893 by Rudolf Diesel. It is a four-stroke engine, like a petrol-fed engine, but it uses a different fuel and ignites it in a different way. When a gas is compressed, it heats up. If a gassy mixture of fuel and air is compressed enough, it will ignite and burn. A diesel engine does not have spark plugs to ignite its fuel; it compresses the fuel instead.

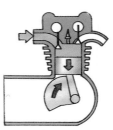

1. Fuel-air sucked in

2. Piston squashes fuel-air mixture

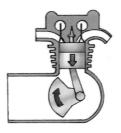

3. Mixture ignited

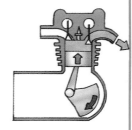

4. Waste gases forced out

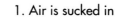

1. Air is sucked in

2. Piston squashes air

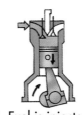

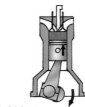

3. Fuel is injected and ignites

4. Waste gases forced out

JETS AND ROCKETS

Two types of engines have been developed for high-power, high-speed vehicles. They are the gas turbine or jet engine, and the rocket. Both of them burn fuel smoothly and continuously instead of in separate bursts as in the piston engine. The jet engine produces a jet of hot gas. The jet itself can propel an aircraft. It can also be used to drive a propeller, as in the turboprop engine, or spin a shaft, as in the turboshaft engine used by helicopters. But jet engines are useless in the airless vacuum of outer space because they need oxygen from the air to burn their fuel. Rocket engines work in space because they carry the oxygen they need with them.

Stabilizing fin

Heat shield

The jet engine

The jet engine was developed in Britain and Germany during World War II. The Gloster E28/39 was one of the first jet aircraft. In a jet engine, air is sucked into the engine and compressed. Fuel is then sprayed in and burned to produce a jet of gas from the back. Turbojets use this jet for propulsion. Airliners use turbofan engines. A fan blows air around a small jet in the middle.

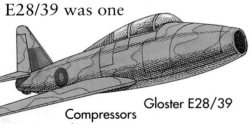

Gloster E28/39

Compressors

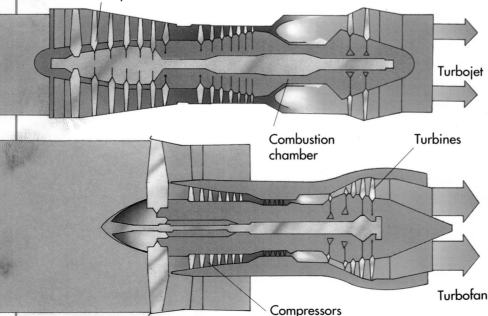

Turbojet

Combustion chamber

Turbines

Compressors

Turbofan

The rocket engine

Most of the space inside a rocket is taken up by tanks containing fuel and oxidizer. Fuel is a substance that burns easily, such as hydrogen, kerosene or, in the case of the European rocket *Ariane*, a chemical containing hydrogen called UDMH (Unsymmetrical DiMethyl Hydrazine). The oxidizer is oxygen, or a substance such as nitrogen tetroxide that contains oxygen. Both the fuel

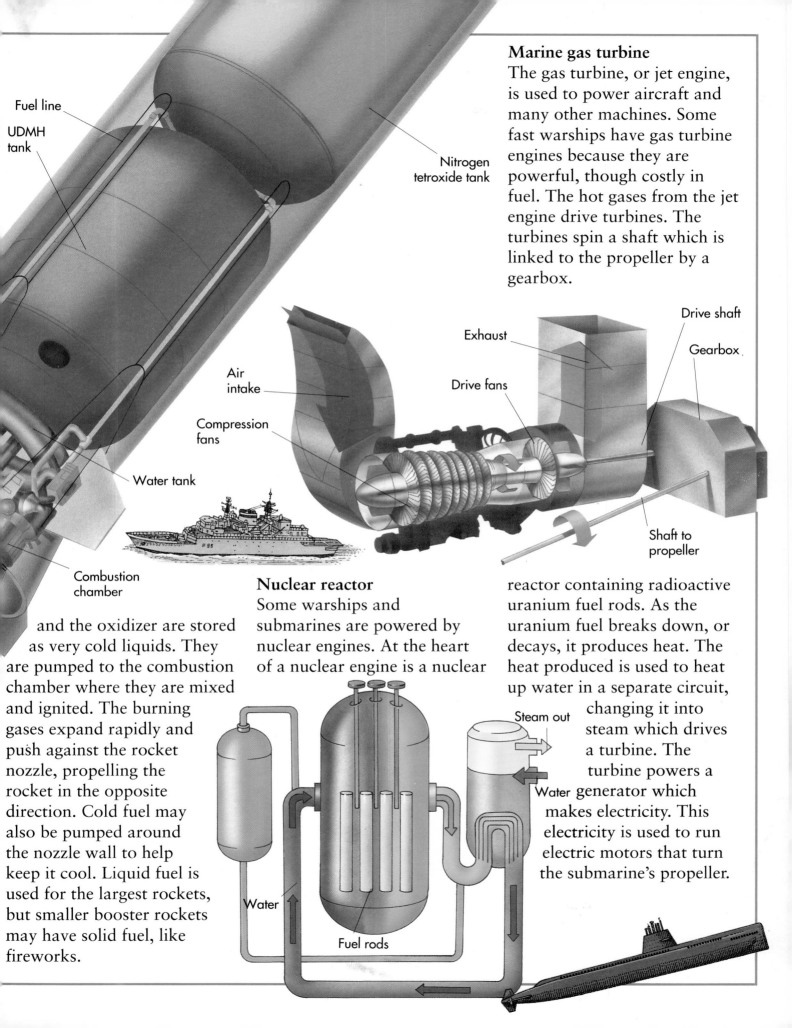

Fuel line

UDMH tank

Nitrogen tetroxide tank

Air intake

Compression fans

Water tank

Combustion chamber

Exhaust

Drive fans

Drive shaft

Gearbox

Shaft to propeller

Marine gas turbine
The gas turbine, or jet engine, is used to power aircraft and many other machines. Some fast warships have gas turbine engines because they are powerful, though costly in fuel. The hot gases from the jet engine drive turbines. The turbines spin a shaft which is linked to the propeller by a gearbox.

and the oxidizer are stored as very cold liquids. They are pumped to the combustion chamber where they are mixed and ignited. The burning gases expand rapidly and push against the rocket nozzle, propelling the rocket in the opposite direction. Cold fuel may also be pumped around the nozzle wall to help keep it cool. Liquid fuel is used for the largest rockets, but smaller booster rockets may have solid fuel, like fireworks.

Nuclear reactor
Some warships and submarines are powered by nuclear engines. At the heart of a nuclear engine is a nuclear reactor containing radioactive uranium fuel rods. As the uranium fuel breaks down, or decays, it produces heat. The heat produced is used to heat up water in a separate circuit, changing it into steam which drives a turbine. The turbine powers a generator which makes electricity. This electricity is used to run electric motors that turn the submarine's propeller.

Steam out

Water

Water

Fuel rods

NAVIGATION

In ancient times, few people ventured further than the next town, perhaps to take animals to market. But when merchants and explorers set out on long journeys, they often had to travel through unfamiliar territory. When they embarked on long sea voyages, they could be out of sight of land, with no landmarks to guide them for months at a time. They developed navigation methods based on what they could see—the sun, moon and stars.

Fore-staff

The astrolabe

Astronomers used an astrolabe to measure the height of stars above the horizon. Travellers and sailors also used it to measure the height of the sun in the sky. This told them how far north they were.

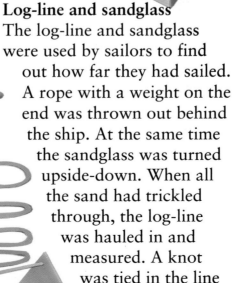

Sand-glass

Log-line and sandglass

The log-line and sandglass were used by sailors to find out how far they had sailed. A rope with a weight on the end was thrown out behind the ship. At the same time the sandglass was turned upside-down. When all the sand had trickled through, the log-line was hauled in and measured. A knot was tied in the line

The fore-staff

The fore-staff was used by early navigators to measure the angle between the sun and the horizon. Using this information, navigators could work out where they were.

every 14.4 metres, so the ship's speed was measured in knots.

Magnetic compass

The compass is an important navigational aid because its magnetized needle always points in the same direction, north, wherever in the world the compass is. The Chinese were the first people to use a compass for navigation, from about AD1000.

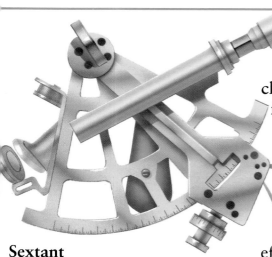

Sextant

The sextant was invented in 1730. It has a mirror which allows the observer to look at the horizon and a reflection of the sun or a star. The angle between the sun or star and the horizon appears on the scale at the bottom.

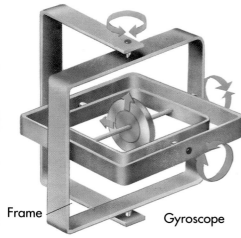

Frame   Gyroscope

Gyroscope navigation

A gyroscope is a heavy wheel. Once it is spinning, it stays in the same position. When it is mounted in a frame that can swivel, the gyroscope stays in the same position while the ship, plane or submarine moves. Three gyroscopes are used to register turning movements. Combining all this information gives the craft's position.

Satellite navigation

When a police car with its siren on races closer to you, the frequency (pitch) of its note rises. When it passes by, the pitch falls again. This change in pitch is called the 'Doppler effect'. Radio waves behave in the same way. Ships use the Doppler effect from satellites to calculate their position.

Aircraft navigation

Some military aircraft, such as the *Tornado*, have automatic navigation systems to allow the plane to fly very low over land. A radio beam keeps the aircraft at the same height as it hugs the contours of hills and valleys. Passenger aircraft use two main navigational aids: radio beacons which transmit from the ground, and signals from satellites.

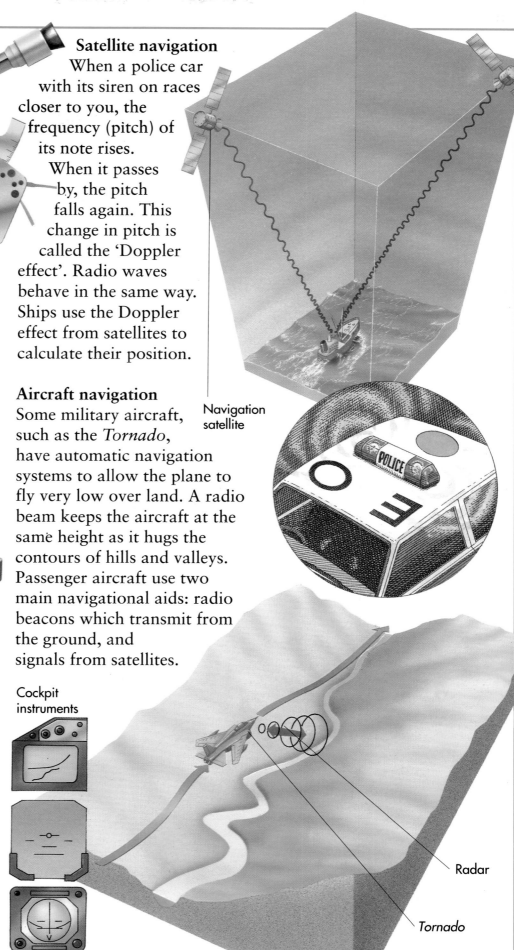

Navigation satellite

Cockpit instruments

Radar

Tornado

SPACE FLIGHT

The 'Space Age' began on 4 October 1957, when the former Soviet Union launched the first artificial satellite, *Sputnik 1*, into orbit around the earth. Other Soviet and American satellites followed, exploring the space around the earth. The first manned spacecraft proved that human beings could survive a space flight and return safely to earth. Each new series of spacecraft and satellite has become more advanced. Deep space probes have also been sent out to explore distant planets.

V-2 rockets

The modern rocket was developed by German scientists and engineers during World War II to bomb London. The V-2 rocket was a fearsome weapon. It was

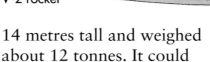

V-2 rocket

14 metres tall and weighed about 12 tonnes. It could carry one tonne of explosives a distance of up to 275km.

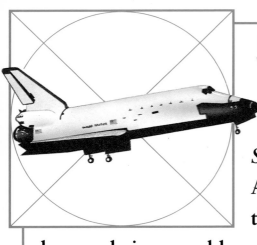

Sputnik 1

A-class booster

Vanguard

Juno 1

Early rockets

The first satellite, *Sputnik 1*, was launched by a Soviet A-class booster. But the booster was not powerful enough for the *Vostok* space capsule, which weighed 4.7 tonnes, so an extra stage was added, transforming it into an A-1 rocket. In America, the development of a new launcher for the *Vanguard* satellite proved unsuccessful. A team of German scientists had more success developing the V-2 into the *Redstone*, *Jupiter C* and *Juno* rockets.

First man in space

On 12 April 1961 a Russian pilot, Yuri Gagarin, climbed into his *Vostok* (meaning 'east') space capsule. The capsule was a sphere 2.5 metres across, covered with heat-shield material. Eleven minutes after his A-1 launch rocket fired, he was in orbit. He had become the first human being to travel beyond the atmosphere and orbit the earth. His capsule made one orbit rising to a height of 327km before ploughing back into the atmosphere. At a height of 7000 metres, Gagarin was ejected from the capsule, and landed by parachute.

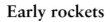

Mercury and Gemini

The United States' answer to *Vostok* was *Mercury*, a series of one-man capsules. After several test flights, *Mercury 6* put the first American, John Glenn, into orbit on 20 February 1962. The next step was *Gemini*, a larger two-man craft. *Gemini* was designed to locate rockets and other spacecraft, manoeuvre around them and dock with them. These operations would be needed for later moon-landing flights.

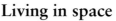
Gemini

Mercury

Vostok 1
1961

Probes

The first satellites carried instruments to study the atmosphere and space near the earth. Electricity to power their instruments was made from sunlight by solar panels. In the 1950s and 1960s, space probes visited the moon, Mercury, Venus and Mars. In the 1970s, two *Pioneer* probes and two *Voyager* probes were sent on a tour of the outer planets. They flew so far from the sun that there was not enough light to use solar panels to make electricity. Instead, they carried their own small nuclear power generators.

Living in space

Life on board a space station such as the Russian *Mir* station (in orbit since 1986) is very different from life on earth. The cosmonauts float from place to place. There is no up or down. Without gravity to work against, the crew's muscles would waste if they did not exercise regularly. The station is supplied with fuel, air, water and food by unmanned, battery-powered spacecraft that fly from earth.

Voyager

Space
station Mir

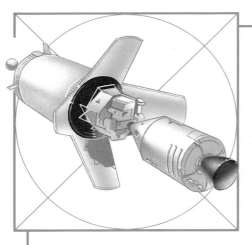

FLYING TO THE MOON

The *Apollo* spacecraft that carried astronauts to the moon consisted of three modules, each with a different job to do. The three-man crew controlled the spacecraft from the command module. For most of the mission, the command module was linked to a service module equipped with a rocket engine. The moon landing was made with a strange spider-like craft called the lunar excursion module (LEM).

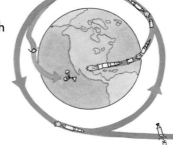

Command module

Crew compartment

Engine nozzle

Main propellant tanks

Service module

Launch vehicle
The *Apollo* spacecraft was launched by a *Saturn 5* rocket. It had three stages. The five rocket engines of the first stage (A) lifted the craft off the ground. At a height of about 50km, the first stage dropped away and the second stage (B) took over. At 160km, this second stage dropped away and the third stage (C) boosted the spacecraft (D) into orbit. If anything had gone wrong during the launch, an escape tower (E) would have pulled the command module to safety.

The command module
Apollo's control centre, the command module, was a tiny cone-shaped craft only 3.9m across the base and 3.6m high. With the crew on board, it weighed only 5.9 tonnes. This tiny module was the only part of the massive *Apollo-Saturn 5* structure to return to earth.

It was supplied with oxygen and power by a service module. Together they formed the command and service module (CSM).

Earth

Heat shield

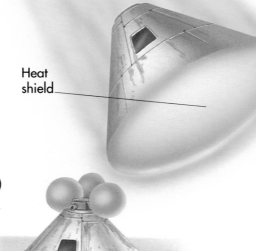

Re-entry
On its return, the command module plunged into the earth's atmosphere. As the air rubbed against the command module a heat-shield on its blunt end protected it from melting. It descended on parachutes to splash down in the ocean.

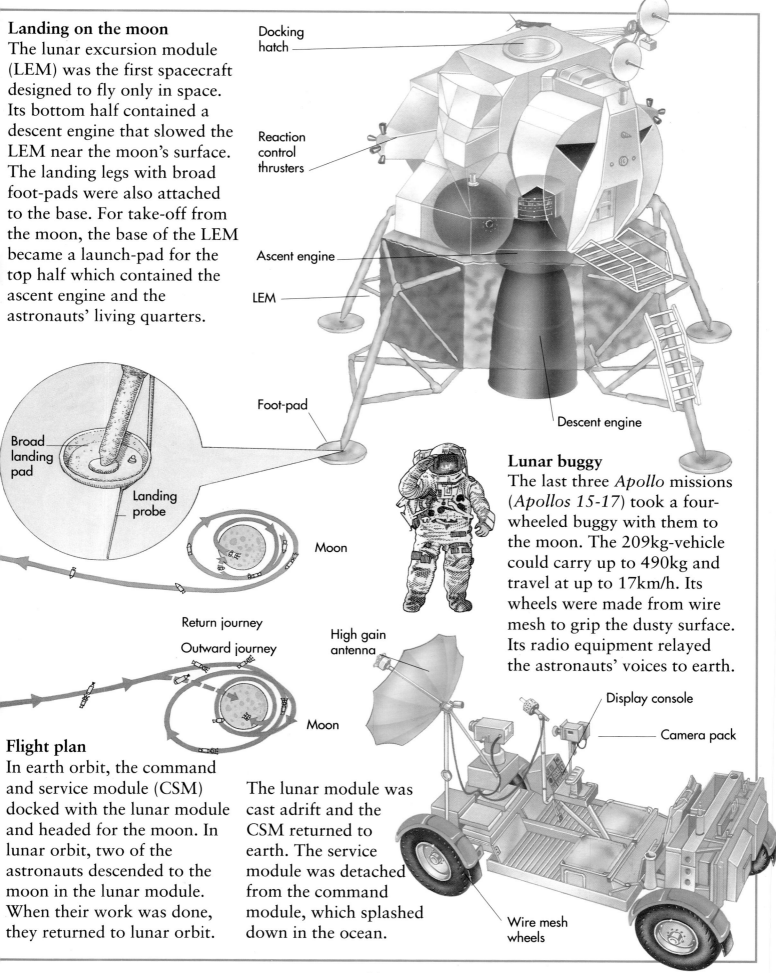

Landing on the moon

The lunar excursion module (LEM) was the first spacecraft designed to fly only in space. Its bottom half contained a descent engine that slowed the LEM near the moon's surface. The landing legs with broad foot-pads were also attached to the base. For take-off from the moon, the base of the LEM became a launch-pad for the top half which contained the ascent engine and the astronauts' living quarters.

Docking hatch

Reaction control thrusters

Ascent engine

LEM

Foot-pad

Descent engine

Broad landing pad

Landing probe

Moon

Return journey

Outward journey

High gain antenna

Moon

Lunar buggy

The last three *Apollo* missions (*Apollos 15-17*) took a four-wheeled buggy with them to the moon. The 209kg-vehicle could carry up to 490kg and travel at up to 17km/h. Its wheels were made from wire mesh to grip the dusty surface. Its radio equipment relayed the astronauts' voices to earth.

Display console

Camera pack

Flight plan

In earth orbit, the command and service module (CSM) docked with the lunar module and headed for the moon. In lunar orbit, two of the astronauts descended to the moon in the lunar module. When their work was done, they returned to lunar orbit.

The lunar module was cast adrift and the CSM returned to earth. The service module was detached from the command module, which splashed down in the ocean.

Wire mesh wheels

THE SPACE SHUTTLE

Until the 1980s, everything that was sent into space was launched by rockets that were used once and thrown away. This was very wasteful. The US Space Shuttle, first launched in 1981, is the first reusable spacecraft. Designing a vehicle that had to be a combination of aircraft and spacecraft posed difficult problems. The shape of the Space Shuttle was designed to survive re-entry and to be able to fly in the earth's atmosphere.

X-24A

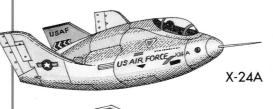

M2F3

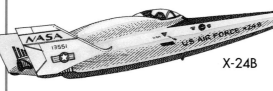

X-24B

Solid rocket boosters

The solid rocket boosters (SRBs) provide extra thrust to launch the Space Shuttle. Each booster stands 45 metres high by 3.8 metres across and weighs 590 tonnes. The two boosters fire for the first two minutes of a flight. At a height of 45km, they fall away from the orbiter and descend under parachutes into the Atlantic Ocean. They are collected by ships and refilled with fuel for another flight.

Lifting bodies

In the 1960s and '70s a series of wingless aircraft called lifting bodies were built to test designs for the Space Shuttle orbiter. They were launched in mid-air from beneath the wing of a B-52 bomber. The fastest lifting bodies could reach a height of 27,500 metres at a speed of almost 2000km/h.

Orbiter
(reusable)

SRB
(reusable)

The orbiter

The orbiter is 37 metres long with a wingspan of 24 metres, the size of a small airliner. It can transport a payload of up to 29.5 tonnes to orbit in its payload bay. The bay is big enough to carry several satellites or a fully equipped space laboratory. The orbiter is powered at take-off by three main engines.

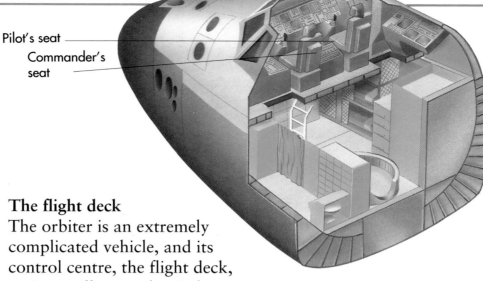

Pilot's seat

Commander's seat

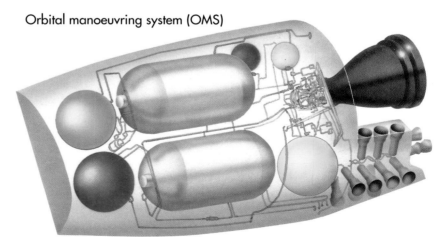

Rocket thrusters

Orbiter nose

The flight deck

The orbiter is an extremely complicated vehicle, and its control centre, the flight deck, is equally complex. It has more than 2000 separate displays and controls. The commander and pilot fly the orbiter with the help of all these displays and controls. The commander sits in the left seat. A mission specialist and up to four payload specialists can be carried too, to look after the orbiter's payloads.

Moving the orbiter

In space, the Shuttle orbiter uses two different propulsion systems to manoeuvre. The rear-pointing orbital manoeuvring system (OMS) engines boost the craft into orbit, move it up and down, and, with the orbiter flying tail first, slow it down to prepare it for landing. Smaller changes in speed and direction are made by 44 rocket thrusters contained in three modules – one in the craft's nose and one in each of two pods on either side of its tail.

Orbital manoeuvring system (OMS)

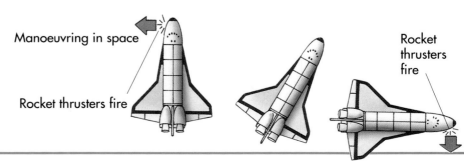

Manoeuvring in space

Rocket thrusters fire

Rocket thrusters fire

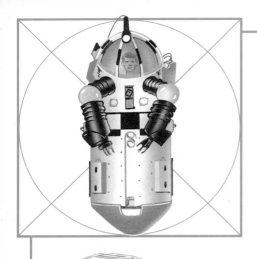

SPECIAL VEHICLES

Most vehicles can be used in a wide range of different conditions. Cars, for example, are designed to be driven on roads, but they can also be driven on dirt tracks, grass and loose gravel. But there are some situations which are so difficult that a vehicle has to be specially designed to cope with them. Most cars and boats do not work well in icy conditions. Most boats cannot be used in very shallow water. And spaceflight involves such extreme conditions that completely new vehicles are needed.

Rudder

Aircraft propeller

OTSO

Airboats

Boats cannot normally be used in places where the water is very shallow or full of weed, because their propellers would hit the bottom or get tangled in the weed. However, in the Everglades swamps at the southern tip of Florida in the United States, the water is both shallow and full of weed. Flat-bottomed boats driven by an aircraft propeller are used in the swamps. They are steered by means of rudders positioned behind the propeller.

Tractors

Farm tractors have to operate reliably on roads, grass, ploughed fields and mud. To

grip loose or wet ground, their tyres have a deep, coarse tread that digs into the ground. The rear wheels, driven by the engine, are much bigger than car wheels. This is because big wheels roll over bumps and hollows more smoothly and easily than small wheels. Tractors need powerful engines to tow heavy machinery. The tractor's engine may also be used to power this machinery.

Modern tractors have covered driving cabs to keep the weather out, and a roll cage around the driver for protection if the tractor should roll over.

Icebreakers

Many important ports are so far north that the sea freezes for part of the year. Icebreaking ships are used to force their way through the ice. An icebreaker's bows are shaped so that the ship rides up on the edge of the ice until its weight shatters the ice. The hull of an icebreaker is strengthened with steel plates.

Skidoos

In areas where there is often deep snow, vehicles called skidoos are used to transport people and goods. The skidoo's weight is supported by ski-like skids. A wheel or caterpillar track underneath the skidoo pushes back against the snow, propelling the skidoo forwards.

Manned manoeuvring unit

Space Shuttle astronauts who have to work around the orbiter move around in space by using a Manned Manoeuvring Unit (MMU). The MMU is a one-person spacecraft: a back-pack propelled by gas jets and controlled by the astronaut. When the astronaut operates the controls at the ends of the arms, nitrogen gas sprays out of one or more of 24 nozzles positioned around the MMU, pushing it in the opposite direction.

MMU

Propellant tanks

Propulsion nozzles

Hand controls

All-terrain vehicles

Most vehicles are designed to travel on roads. If they drive off the road on to muddy earth or loose gravel, their tyres find it more difficult to grip the surface. All-terrain vehicles are designed to cope with almost any conditions. They have more than four wheels with soft tyres for extra grip. The bottom of the vehicle is sealed so that it can drive through water.

INDEX